The Wiri Wiri Peppers ® at the Fruit and Vegetable Commonwealth Games in London.

A little fairy story by Ruthy Richards-Levi © 2017.

All rights reserved. No part of this publication may be reproduced, stored in a retrieval system, or transmitted in any form or by any means, electronic, mechanical, photocopying, recording or otherwise, without prior written permission of the author and illustrator.

A Catalogue record for this book is available from The British Library.
ISBN:978-19996464-5-5
Cover design by Ruthy Richards-Levi
Back cover photograph reproduced with kind permission of Mrs Lynette Richards-Lorde©.

For My Granny and Grandad
Beatrice Eudora Richards-Browne and John Augustus Richards aka (J.R)
Who are always there for little me. Love Always x.

Once upon a time, in a far-away land in South America, a little to the North there lay a magical land called Guyana. A quaint and cosy place where different peoples, creatures, and flora of many sorts and species lived in abundance and harmony. There was much excitement everywhere because it was the first time they would take part in the Fruit and Vegetable Commonwealth Games in London.

Now this land had some of the most exquisite and most delicious foods in the world, and this meant they had to choose who will represent them at the Fruit and Vegetable Commonwealth Games. Extra care had to be taken on account of the fact that only one plane ticket was available a kind and generous donation from Yummies Partnership.

Competitions of all kinds were held locally in districts, towns, rural areas and villages to help decide who will be chosen for the Commonwealth Games. In the end, finally one of the tiniest vegetables was chosen to represent The Co-operative Republic of Guyana: The lucky ones were to be the WiriWiri they would showcase just a bit of what was so amazing about this magical land.

Perhaps some of you are wondering "What is a Wiri Wiri Pepper"

Well Wiri Wiri is a member of the Capsicum Family, and many of you know their more famous relatives, the Big Bell Peppers and Long Tall Chilli Peppers.

In Guyana, the super-hot little Wiri Wiri berries peppers live most of their lives on their Mummy and Daddy bushes in the Amerindian Jungle deep in the hinterland.

page 4

The Head Amerindian Chief, officially known as Chief Owen was assigned to choose the very best species of Wiri Wiris to be ambassadors for Guyana and take pride at the Commonwealth Games. He chose six in all for six different shades of colour that fell within the red, pink, orange, green and yellow colour range.

Pleased as punch he quietly whispered to his wife Evangeline, "They represent each of the peoples of our magical land:

Amerindian, African, Chinese, European, Indian and Portuguese. I am very proud of them."

So, the six chosen tiny Wiri Wiri friends began their 10,000-km journey to London, England. First from their home in the Deep Amerindian jungle they journeyed to the Capital city of Georgetown by trail, river and road.

On their way, they passed many fantastical wonders. They basked happily in the cool shadow of Mount Roraima; they stood in awe of the might of the majestic Kaieteur Waterfall, and they traversed across the wide-open savannah lands of the hilly sand belt that stretches from the Rupununi to Demerara.

After arriving in Georgetown, they greeted the kind crowds of the market stall holders and citizens wishing them well at Stabroek Market. Later they had a ride in the motor cade from the President and First Lady to Goedverwagteng and Ogle Airport.

Everyone was there waving them off to success. All the other competitors for the ticket were there too and they was only good will….no jealousy just smiles.

The Mangoes and the Pineapples made smoothies for them and the Cassava and Eddoes made delicious pepper pot packed lunches for the long flight overseas.

When the Wiri Wiris boarded the Carico Airlines Plane they sat in 1A. Being so tiny they could all fit on one seat. It was their first time on a plane. After take-off, they undid their seat belt and climbed up on the window sill to see the wide world spread beneath them.

Captain Mike Simon came to see them on board and gave them a special announcement and let them see the cockpit too. He would take them as far as Barbados where he would personally hand them over to his friend and colleague the Captain Elon on British Airways. They would fly directly to London's Gatwick Airport …. What super fun! In London, the High Commissioner welcomed them heartily and took the Wiri Wiri's on a tour.

In London, The High Commissioner for Guyana in England took them to the Tower of London, the Houses of Parliament, Windsor Castle, the London Eye, Oxford Street and Buckingham Palace. They even got their photographs taken with the Guards outside the Palace and high tea at The Goring Hotel, they really enjoyed themselves. After seeing all the tourist sights the prepared themselves and got ready for the games….

They all wore cute little uniforms embroidered with the colours of the Golden Arrowhead, Guyana's flag. Their stalks were used as canes for walking, and each of them had a shiny leaf hat on his or her head. Together, they looked super smart and cool.

The opening ceremony in London was opened by HRH Her Majesty The Queen and was a great spectacle. The games began with a procession of all the countries of the Commonwealth Participating. The Wiri Wiri's were the smallest team and the last of the G-Group of countries to enter the massive stadium. The marched quite proudly with the Golden Arrowhead Flag unfurled in front of them. Everyone back home form the Deep Amerindian Jungle to the towns and villages listened to the radio and watched the events on the TV with great anticipation. There was even a live stream for viewers on internet. They were seen around the globe.

Their event was "The hottest pepper" and the little Wiri Wiris desperately wanted to win. The other peppers in the competition were much bigger than them but all were kind except one called Shaun who was a bully and was mean taunting them and laughing at their funny way of walking on their leaf feet ….but the others Capsicums rallied round and he was punished by the judges …he later apologised to them.

The Wiri Wiris were not discouraged. Instead they just became even more determined and emboldened and forthright as the time drew closer.

Their event required them to be tested to see which of all the peppers was the hottest in the World. There was a professional taster, a gentleman –all decked out in a polka dot bow-tie and chic suit whose take it was to taste each pepper in oil. No pepper was to be chewed or swallowed. Just their essences were to be tasted.

First up was the bell pepper….they were not hot at all! They Lost! Next in Line was the Canadian team with huge Red Peppers .Its chance of winning was slim as they came from the colder Northern climates. Then their cousins The Chillies grown in Australia ,were next. After tasting there was a stir of curiosity and interest on the judge's face ,but it soon faded. They too failed to impress.

At last it was the Wiri Wiri's turn: And it lasted just seconds! The Judge's face turned scarlet! His eyes welled up and he began to cry out, " The winner is Wiri Wiri of Guyana! Please give me some Milk! I am
Burning up! Milk, Water Pleease….he sighed in surprise wringing his hands he smiled at the winners the little Wiri Wiri's. Everyone cheered!

The Whole of Guyana and Guyanese in the diaspora all over the world screamed in joy and amazement!
The stadium erupted in deafening shouts and cheers for the tiny unassuming Wiri Wiris.

As the six of them stood on the podium to receive their Commonwealth Golden Medals and flowers, they held their little green leaf hands together waving, all crying tears of joy and smiling.

The Wiri Wiris had pit Guyana on the Map! This was the nation's first ever Gold Medal at a Commonwealth Fames for Fruit and Vegetables and they would now be famous the world over-known as the hottest Pepper officially in the whole world.

And this is how it came to be that today the Wiri Wiri is now available exclusively in the very best stores, such as Fortnum and Mason in London, Whole Foods in America and even in Hong Kong and of course countless markets and supermarkets across the lands of the Caribbean and Africa.

Now I guess you are wondering what happened to our winning team? All six of the Wiri Wiri champions lived happily ever after. They married and had their own families of little Wiri Wiri's and they were always ready to tell the tale of how they had represented Guyana and won the highest honour and the most prestigious Gold Medal of the Commonwealth Games in London.

The End of the Story ☺Ruthy Richards-Levi ©

Thank you hope you enjoyed this book. Do look out for more adventures and stories from Ruthy

Rrl613@gmail.com

Glossary:

Amerindian – The original inhabitants of the Guyana Regions.

Commonwealth - A wonderful intergovernmental organisation of 53 member countries working together for the public welfare of all the peoples and for the common good.

Evangeline - Geek Name bringer of good news.

Goedverwagteng - An Old Dutch place name meaning Good expectations.

Wiri Wiri –  Capsicum pepper extremely hot and extremely small….

Dear friends

Thank you for choosing this little book..... The wiri wiri is synonymous with the land of Guyana and in this story the little wiri wiri's represent the 6 nationalities that have their home in the Land of Many Rivers that is Guyana.

Enjoy
love Raffey

The author & illustrator aged 2 with Family in 47 Palm Street Georgetown Guyana circa 1966.

Made in the USA
Lexington, KY
28 March 2018